PENGUIN

T0118924

Exploring Southeast Asia with Liu Kang: Master of Colour

Eva Wong Nava is an award-winning children's book author. She writes picture books to entertain, engage, and enthral young readers. She is also an art historian. When not writing for children, she meanders art museums and galleries waiting for the next piece of art work to speak to her and inspire another story. She weaves stories from art at *CarpeArte* Journal. When not writing, Eva teaches the art of picture book creation through her workshops under the brand, Picture Book Matters. Eva can be found on Twitter, Instagram and Facebook engaging people in conversations about art and stories.

Jeffrey Say is an art historian specialising in Singapore and Southeast Asian art history. Jeffrey has been instrumental in the development of art history studies at LASALLE College of the Arts, supporting artists to develop a contextual and historical understanding of the evolution of visual arts. In 2009, he designed the world's first Master's programme focussing on Asian modern and contemporary art histories. Jeffrey is a public advocate of the importance of art history to Singapore. He is a frequent public speaker at museums, universities and galleries, and conducts short courses which remain hugely popular among various publics. Jeffrey is also a regular commentator on the local visual arts scene. An author of numerous essays on art, his seminal co- edited work *Histories, Practices, Interventions: A Reader in Singapore Contemporary Art* (2016) remains a critical anthology for researchers, curators and students on Singapore art to date.

Quek Hong Shin is a Singaporean freelance author and illustrator whose works include picture books like *The Amazing Sarong*, *The Brilliant Oil Lamp and Universe of Feelings*. *The Incredible Basket*, was the winner of Best Children's Book at the 2019 Singapore Book Awards. He is also the illustrator for other children's titles like *The One and Only Inuka* and the *Ahoy, Navy!* series that was published in celebration of the Republic of Singapore Navy's 50th Anniversary in 2017.

PENGUIN BOOKS

USA | Canada | UK | Ireland | Australia
New Zealand | India | South Africa | China | Southeast Asia

Penguin Books is part of the Penguin Random House group
of companies whose addresses can be found at global.
penguinrandomhouse.com

Published by Penguin Random House SEA Pte Ltd
9, Changi South Street 3, Level 08-01,
Singapore 486361

Penguin
Random House
SEA

First published in Penguin Books by Penguin Random House
SEA 2022

ISBN 9789814954365

www.penguin.sg

EXPLORING SOUTHEAST ASIA WITH

LIU KANG

MASTER OF COLOUR

Eva Wong Nava and Jeffrey Say

Illustrated by Quek Hong Shin

PENGUIN BOOKS

An imprint of Penguin Random House

One day, while strolling along the streets of Singapore, Liu Kang came to a kampung where he saw a river flow.

Liu Kang's eyes soaked in the colours around him.

2

The luscious greens of the trees.
  The multi-coloured shades of the women's sarongs.
    The tinge of blue flowing through the village.

This explosion of colours made Liu Kang giddy with joy.
  He couldn't believe that such beauty could be found
  at home.

Liu Kang was captivated by the vibrant colours of life in this kampung and returned many times to paint it. He was thrilled that rustic villages like this could be found in modern Singapore. By this time, Liu Kang had already painted many of Singapore's sights and scenes. But the way he painted this village was special.

5

He sketched the wooden houses on stilts. He combined his knowledge of Chinese traditional painting with batik, a type of fabric art.

He drew the trees with large verdant leaves. He used strong outlines and flat surfaces seen in Chinese paintings and filled the spaces inside the lines with vibrant colours made from oil.

He painted the people in their native clothes. In this manner, Liu Kang found a way to modernize Chinese paintings.

As an artist trained in Western-style paintings and someone who liked painting outdoors, Liu Kang found the street scenes in Singapore captivating. A building site caught his attention. There he saw émigré Chinese women hard at work.

He painted the Samsui women with their heads clad in a red scarf .

He painted them in their rubber sandals with trousers folded up to their knees.

He painted them ferrying baskets of sand up and down wooden planks.

Once, not so long ago, when Singapore was ruled by the British, Liu Kang had thought that the island was an arid land, without beauty. He missed China, his homeland, where mythical mountains peaked out of fluffy clouds and ancient rivers flowed freely.

He wrote down his thoughts and shared them with his painter friends. He told them of the need to find a new way to make Chinese art. Liu Kang was proud of traditional Chinese painting but he knew that this way of art-making had to change for the future generation to be able to embrace art.

Although Singapore had many interesting scenes for Liu Kang to explore and paint, he had one secret desire.

Liu Kang wanted to be like the French artist, Paul Gauguin, who painted the landscape and people in Tahiti. He wanted to blend the exotic with the modern.

But French Polynesia was too far away.
    And money was tight.
        The war had made travelling anywhere impossible.

Then, in 1952, when the Second World War was long over,
Liu Kang made his way to an island not far from Singapore.
He was accompanied by three other painter friends, all
eager to capture the natural beauty outdoors.

Liu Kang found his paradise in Bali.

His hands traced the architectural lines of the temples.
   Touching these ancient stones made his heart sing.
      Being surrounded by a mystical aura cleared his mind.

Liu Kang couldn't believe that such exotic beauty could be
found so close to home.

15

Strolling down the streets of Bali, Liu Kang observed how artistic the Balinese were.

They danced gracefully.
They sculpted artistically.
They played complex tunes on the gamelan.

Nature is an artist's greatest teacher

'This feels like a dream,' he said aloud.
He sketched and he sketched.
He painted all the beauty he found around him.

The natural landscape mystified Liu Kang.
    The romantic ambiance in Bali opened up his senses.
        The spiritual surroundings allowed his mind to
        roam free.

'Nature is an artist's greatest teacher,' he thought.

Here in Bali, he drew lines with his brush.
In Bali, Liu Kang blended both East and West.
There in Bali, he found a new way to paint.

I paint with western materials and tools, but my style and substance are Chinese. This is a happy medium for me.

19

When Liu Kang returned to Singapore, a new style emerged.

He began to see the island of Singapore through a different lens.

He marvelled at the natural beauty of his island-home.

Liu Kang painted people at work and at play. He observed the animals among the people and painted them too.

Liu Kang painted running rivers and he filled his canvas with pops of colours. These colours made nature come alive.

Liu Kang painted the luscious landscape of Singapore. He blended Western techniques with Eastern aesthetics.

This way of making art gave Liu Kang immense pleasure.

By painting the people and
landscape in the open-air,
Liu Kang found his homeland.
He no longer missed China
as much.

By walking through the fields and villages of Singapore, he could absorb the cultural atmosphere of the land.

By watching the locals at work and play, he drank in the multicultural elements of Nanyang, the Southern Seas.

As the years went by, Liu Kang no longer felt that Singapore was an island devoid of beauty. He discovered different kampungs to sketch and paint. He observed the diversity of the people, which he coloured to life. His nose began to recognize the various floral perfumes of the land as his eyes took in all their multi-coloured hues.

Liu Kang documented all these sensory
influences in more than one thousand
pieces of artwork. He continued to paint
in the Nanyang style until his death.

Liu Kang finally
believed that
such exotic
beauty could be
found at home.

Who is Liu Kang?

Liu Kang was born in Fujian, China, in 1911. He spent his early years in Malaya (now Singapore and Malaysia) under the British government, where his father worked as a rubber merchant. He was named Liu Kai at birth but a mispronunciation of his name at his school in Muar, Malaysia, led to him being known as Liu Kang. Liu Kang studied art at the Xinhua Art Academy in Shanghai and at the Académie de la Grande Chaumière in Paris. In Paris, he was inspired by the work of post-Impressionist artists such as Paul Cézanne, Paul Gauguin, and Vincent Van Gogh. In Shanghai, he was influenced by Liu Haisu (they are not related), who was one of the four pioneers of modern Chinese art. When the Chinese invaded China in 1937, Liu Kang moved to

Muar and then to Singapore. When Japan invaded Singapore in 1942, he and his family fled back to Muar, leaving behind more than 200 paintings, which were never recovered. He decided to settle permanently in Singapore after the war. Malaya and the region of Southeast Asia was known as Nanyang ('Southern Seas') to the mainland Chinese as it was situated to the south of China. In his artistic style, Liu Kang integrated influences from Chinese and Western aesthetics but the subject matter for his paintings was drawn from the Nanyang region. As a result, the style developed by Liu Kang and some of his contemporaries has become popularly known as the Nanyang style or the Nanyang movement.

Liu Kang
Life by the River, 1975
Oil on canvas, 126 x 203 cm
Gift of the artist. Collection of National Gallery Singapore.

Liu Kang painted *Life by the River* in 1975, more than twenty years after his visit to Bali. This indicates that Bali really did make an impression on the way Liu Kang painted. Of his entire oeuvre of work, the Nanyang style remains what Liu Kang is most famous for. This oil painting can be found at the National Gallery of Singapore.

Let's Talk About The Artwork

1. What is going on in this painting? What made you say this?

2. What do you think life was like in Singapore at that time? What are the children in the painting doing? What games do you think they might be playing?

3. There are some boats in the river. What do you think these boats are called? Why are they known by this name?

4. Say why you think Liu Kang is known as the 'Master of Colours'. Why do you think he used certain colours in the painting? What do the colours do in the painting?

5. Have you noticed how the painting is labelled? Why is it important to let viewers know the title, size, and medium of the art work?

6. When you visit museums around the world, be sure to take note of how paintings are labelled. Do all museums label the artworks similarly?